Teen Issues

ALCOHOL

Jim Pollard and Chloë Kent

www.raintreepublishers.co.uk
Visit our website to find out more information about **Raintree** books.

To order:
☎ Phone 44 (0) 1865 888113
🖹 Send a fax to 44 (0) 1865 314091
💻 Visit the Raintree Bookshop at **www.raintreepublishers.co.uk** to browse our catalogue and order online.

First published in Great Britain by
Raintree, Halley Court,
Jordan Hill, Oxford OX2 8EJ, part of
Harcourt Education.
Raintree is a registered trademark of Harcourt
Education Ltd.

© Harcourt Education Ltd 2004
First published in paperback in 2005
The moral right of the proprietor has been asserted.

Editorial: Charlotte Guillain
and Kate Buckingham
Design: Michelle Lisseter
and Tinstar Design Ltd (www.tinstar.co.uk)
Picture Research: Mica Brancic
Production: Jonathan Smith
Index: Indexing Specialists (UK) Ltd

Originated by Dot Gradations
Printed and bound in China by South China
Printing Company

ISBN 1 844 43142 8 (hardback)
08 07 06 05 04
10 9 8 7 6 5 4 3 2 1

ISBN 1 844 43149 5 (paperback)
09 08 07 06 05
10 9 8 7 6 5 4 3 2 1

British Library Cataloguing in Publication Data
Pollard, Jim
Alcohol
362.2'92
A full catalogue record for this book is available from
the British Library.

Acknowledgements
The publishers would like to thank the following for
permission to reproduce photographs: Alamy pp.
10–11, 12–13, 14–15, 28–29, 34–35, 38; Christine
Osborne p. 8; Corbis pp. 11, 12, 14, 15, 18–19, 18,
20, 20–21, 22, 22–23, 23, 24, 26–27, 28, 30, 31, 32,
38–39, 39, 41, 42–43, 43, 46–47, 46, 47, 48–49, 49,
50–51, 51; Creatas pp. 4–5, 25, 52–53; Gareth Boden
p. 7; Getty pp. 12, 42, 44–45 (PhotoDisc); Kobal pp.
8–9; KPT Power Photos p. 4; Powerstock pp. 32–33,
36–37, 40–41, 48; SPL pp. 9, 24–25, 35; Stone pp.
6–7 (Paul Harris); Tudor photography pp. i, 14,
16–17, 21, 26, 29, 30–31, 34, 36, 50.

Cover photo of empty wine bottles reproduced with
permission of Robert Harding Picture Library
(Premium Stock).

Every effort has been made to contact copyright
holders of any material reproduced in this book. Any
omissions will be rectified in subsequent printings if
notice is given to the publishers.

The paper used to print this book comes from
sustainable resources.

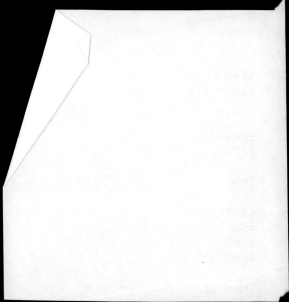

Contents

easy Reading

Any words appearing in the text in bold, **like this**, are explained in the Glossary.
You can also look out for them in the 'In the know' box at the bottom of each page.

The most popular drug

If you want to look after yourself and your body, you need to know the facts. That is what this book is all about.

Q Where does alcohol come from?

A People make alcohol. It can be made from a variety of foods and other ingredients. These foods include apples, grapes, berries, cereals, barley and potatoes.

Here is a question to start with:

Do you know which drug is taken by the most people around the world?

Here are some clues:
• This drug is not an **illegal** drug.
• It is not the sort of drug a doctor might tell you to take, like an aspirin.
• It is not even cigarettes or tobacco.

You might have worked it out already because you have read the title of this book. Alcohol is probably the most popular drug in the world.

Getting the facts

People drink alcohol in nearly every country in the world. In countries like the UK, the USA and Australia, about two people out of three drink alcohol. Like all drugs, alcohol changes the way you feel. And, like all drugs, it can be dangerous if not used properly.

What is alcohol? Why do people drink it? What does it do to our bodies? This book tells you the facts about drinking alcohol so that you can make up your own mind.

Find out later...

What happens to your body when you drink alcohol?

How can alcohol be part of a healthy, happy life?

Why can alcohol be dangerous if you drink too much of it?

What is alcohol?

Most communities in the world have made and drunk alcohol, but not all of them. For example, the aboriginal people of Australia did not drink alcohol until European people came to settle in their country.

Alcohol is a drug. It can be made from all sorts of foods including cereals, apples and grapes. The sugars in these foods are turned into alcohol using yeast. Yeast is the fungus that is also used to make bread. To make alcohol, the food is mixed with yeast and water and left for a while. Gradually, the yeast turns the sugar into alcohol. This is called **fermentation**. There are different ways of making alcoholic drinks, like beer and whisky. These are just different ways of turning the sugars found in food into alcohol.

fermentation   changing sugar to alcohol by adding yeast

How is it made?

Beer is made from cereals, cider is made from apples and wine is made from grapes. Spirits like whisky and vodka are much stronger drinks. Whisky is made from cereals. Vodka is made from grain or potatoes. These are just some examples of foods found around the world that can be made into alcohol.

Mixing drinks

Some alcohol can be mixed with **soft drinks**. You can even mix different types of alcohol to make cocktails. Cocktails can have fantastic names like Harvey Wallbanger or Purple Nasty. Some of these drinks are very expensive, but they are nothing more than ordinary alcohol that has had other things added to it.

Home-made

You do not need a big **brewery** to make alcohol. Many people make wine and beer at home. Home-made wine can be made from almost anything, including dandelions, garlic and even stinging nettles. Some home-made beers and wines taste good – some do not!

◀ The tanks at this whisky **distillery** are used to separate alcohol from water, yeast and other waste.

soft drinks   drinks that do not contain alcohol, like orange juice and cola

Why people drink alcohol

Alcohol is part of our everyday lives. People have been making and drinking it for nearly as long as there have been human beings on the Earth. There are ancient Egyptian writings more than 5500 years old that describe wine making.

Alcohol is often seen as part of relaxing and having a good time. People drink **champagne** or other drinks to celebrate birthdays, weddings and other happy events. All types of television programmes and films show people drinking. In soaps and television comedies, everyone discusses their problems in the local bar.

▲ Christians use red wine in **Holy Communion** because the wine reminds them of the blood of Jesus Christ.

Religion

Alcohol is important in some religions. In other religions like **Islam**, alcohol is not used at all.

Reasons for not drinking

Not everyone drinks alcohol. Some people do not drink for religious reasons. Some people do not drink for health reasons. Others do not drink because they just do not like it. Whether you drink or not, and how much you drink is up to you. It is your choice.

➤➤➤➤➤➤➤➤➤➤➤➤➤➤
Go to pages 42 to 43 to find out more about different religions' attitudes to alcohol.

champagne   fizzy alcoholic drink made from grapes
heroin   powerful and addictive drug

The alcohol in alcoholic drinks goes into your blood, your brain and the rest of your body. This is how it changes the way you feel. Even if you only drink a small amount, you may make mistakes or do or say things you would not normally. To enjoy drinking safely, it is very important to remember the effects alcohol has on your body.

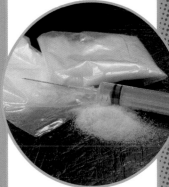

'Alcohol is not as dangerous as drugs.'

FALSE

Used carefully, alcohol is not dangerous. But if it is not used carefully, alcohol can kill. It kills more people than **heroin**. In 2000, **illegal** drugs like heroin killed 223,000 people around the world. In the same year, alcohol killed 1,800,000 people around the world.

▲ When James Bond is not saving the world, he likes to drink a Vodka Martini 'shaken, not stirred'.

Holy Communion   ceremony in which bread and wine are blessed and shared
Islam   the religion of Muslims

Is drinking alcohol fun?

If alcohol changes the way your brain works, why do people drink it at all? Because one of the first changes people notice when they drink alcohol is that they feel more relaxed. If you feel more relaxed, then you feel more comfortable with other people, especially if you are shy or you do not know the other people very well. That is why alcohol is so popular at parties. It helps to make you feel part of the gang.

▼ Alcohol and parties often go together. Do you always need an alcoholic drink to have fun?

In many films, alcohol is used to show how sophisticated certain characters are. James Bond always seems to impress his girlfriends with **champagne** and cocktails. Is this a realistic way of looking at alcohol?

The full story

The trouble is, we often only see the good side of alcohol. Many magazines and television programmes are full of advertisements that show people having fun when they are drinking. That is only half the story. One drink may help someone to relax at a party so that they have more fun. But that does not mean they will have twice as much fun if they have two drinks, or three times as much fun if they have three. It is just not as simple as that. In fact, it is the opposite. Too much alcohol can make you very ill indeed – and that is no fun at all.

Q What is a hangover?

A The morning after drinking alcohol, people often feel ill and have a headache. They may feel very tired because the alcohol has stopped them sleeping properly. Some people are sick. This is called a hangover.

Why start drinking?

There are many reasons why young people start to drink. They want to feel they are part of a group just as much as older people – perhaps more. Younger children often think alcohol tastes horrible, so learning to like it is seen as part of becoming an adult.

▲ It is quite normal for young children in some countries to drink wine mixed with water at meal times.

First drink

These young people all had their first drink for different reasons.

In moderation

In France children often drink a small amount of alcohol. There are fewer problems with alcohol among young people in France than in the UK.

People kept asking me to buy alcohol for them because I looked older. One day I thought I may as well try it.

Getting wrecked on Saturday night is just something you do. It's better than taking drugs.

I started to drink booze because all my mates in the park were drinking. I thought it tasted disgusting, but I felt left out otherwise.

My dad bought me my first drink. It was **lager**, I think. I'd rather have just had lemonade, but drinking it made me feel more grown-up.

age limit   legal age when you can start drinking alcohol

In countries like the USA, the UK and Australia, people probably have their first alcoholic drink when they are teenagers. They might be offered it by an adult or a friend. Some people just accept without thinking. But it makes sense to find out as much as you can about alcohol and to think about its effects before this happens. Then you will know whether you want say 'Yes' or 'No'.

I'll be honest. I'm really shy and it just feels easier to talk to people after I've had a drink.

How problems start

Once alcohol becomes part of your life, it can affect you in lots of different ways. Many people just enjoy it from time to time, but for others the alcohol becomes more important than that. This can cause problems, as Colin found out.

'I remember how it all started really clearly. A driver opened his car door and knocked me off my skateboard. I was really shaken up. My legs felt like rubber and I needed something to calm me down. I knew how a glass of wine could make my dad relax when he was stressed, so I bought some booze. I was floating…I felt great.'

'My parents were really worried about how I was doing at school. Drinking helped me to relax. I'd have a drink and I could do my homework without stressing. The quick drink before homework soon became three drinks before going to bed. I wasn't bothered, although I wasn't sleeping well. Also I had always felt a bit nervous at parties, but now I had a drink before I got there and it was better. But everything changed when I failed my exams – big time. Now there's no time for skateboarding or parties. I've got to revise for retakes.'

Think about this…

Alcohol can make you say things you would not normally say. You might regret saying these things later!

Did I tell you about that time I lost my underpants?

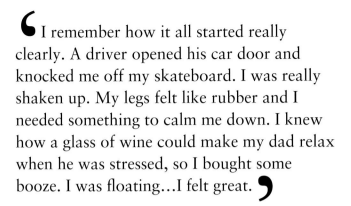

The effects of alcohol

Measures

Drinks come in different sizes around the world. US pints are smaller than pints in other English-speaking countries.

1 US pint = 0.83 UK/Australian pint

How will alcohol affect you? Well, that depends on lots of different things, including how much you drink and how fast you drink it. Some drinks are stronger than others. This means the stronger drinks contain more alcohol than the weaker drinks. Spirits like whisky are about 40 per cent alcohol. Beers usually contain about 5 per cent alcohol.

How do you know how much alcohol is in a drink? Health experts have thought of that. They measure alcoholic drinks in units. A unit is 8 to 10 millilitres of alcohol. The standard drinks sold in bars may all be different sizes, but they usually have about one unit of alcohol in them. You can see by comparing the size of a small whisky with a beer just how much stronger spirits are.

One unit is equal to...

one 25 ml glass of whisky	one 125 ml glass of lower-strength wine	half pint of standard-strength beer (UK)	10 oz ordinary beer (Australia)	12 oz bottle of beer (USA)

optic   something fixed on the top of a bottle so that it pours out the same measure each time

Measuring alcohol

Most bottles and cans tell you how much alcohol they contain. For example, a 33 centilitre can of beer contains about 5 per cent alcohol.

33 cl = 330 ml so you multiply 330 by 0.05.

This equals about 16.

This means there are 16 ml of alcohol in the can, which is nearly two units.

Most bars use a glass measure or an **optic** to make sure the drinks they serve are the right size. But not all countries measure their alcohol as accurately as this. On holiday, you will probably come across some bars that just pour your drink from the bottle without measuring it.

How strong?

Drinks come in different strengths around the world – even drinks that are the same type. A light Australian or American beer may be 3 per cent alcohol or less. A typical European **lager** beer can be as strong as 6 to 8 per cent. This can make it hard to know exactly how much alcohol you are drinking.

Where does it go?

Alcohol reaches your stomach moments after you drink it. Here the alcohol is **absorbed** into the bloodstream and travels around the body to the brain. The alcohol slows down the messages your brain sends to the rest of your body. Alcohol is a **depressant**. It affects the way you think and what you do. You may:

- feel relaxed
- say or do things you normally would not
- feel slightly dizzy
- feel less anxious.

When the alcohol reaches the stomach you may feel hungry or sick. If you have not eaten anything for a while and your stomach is empty, the alcohol will affect you even more.

What happens next...

Alcohol is broken down in the **liver**. It takes the body's liver one hour to break down one unit of alcohol. That means that after one hour, the alcohol will no longer affect you, unless you have had another drink.

Too chilled

Alcohol can make you very relaxed. Often too relaxed to make the right choice.

Let's forget the exam revision and enjoy some more beers in the sunshine.

absorb   soak up
depressant   something that slows you down

Even after one drink it is more difficult to do some things, like driving. In some countries it is **illegal** to drive after drinking any alcohol at all. It is certainly not a good idea to ride a bike or operate machinery. You also should not mix alcohol with other drugs. Drugs given to you by your doctor may not work properly or may be dangerous if mixed with alcohol.

TRUE OR FALSE?

'Eating a big meal before drinking will stop you getting drunk.'

FALSE

A full stomach may mean the alcohol goes into the blood more slowly, but in the end the effects are exactly the same.

▲ It is important to keep in mind all the effects alcohol can have on your body.

liver   part of the body turning nutrients from food and drink into the proteins and sugars the body needs

Alcohol and your body

As well as the short-term effects, alcohol has long-term effects. Some of these can be very dangerous. In fact, drinking a lot regularly can damage every part of the body and can even kill.

Q&A

Q What happens if you keep drinking?

A After two drinks, you are more likely to want to urinate.

After three, you will think more slowly, speak less clearly and be less able to make good decisions.

After four, you will walk less steadily and may not be able to see clearly.

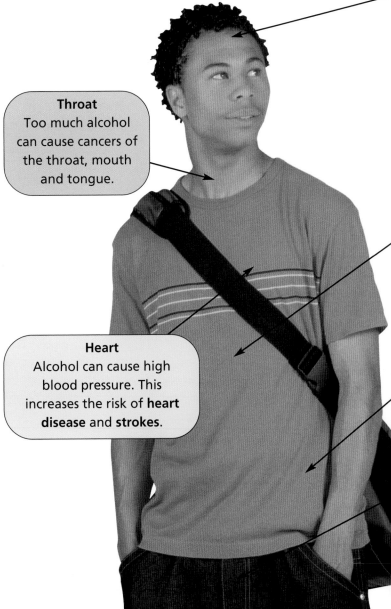

Throat
Too much alcohol can cause cancers of the throat, mouth and tongue.

Heart
Alcohol can cause high blood pressure. This increases the risk of **heart disease** and **strokes**.

cirrhosis   when the liver becomes scarred

Brain
Even a small amount of alcohol can slow the brain down and make you depressed. Over a long time, too much alcohol can cause brain damage.

Stomach
Too much alcohol causes stomach problems like ulcers. Ulcers are open sores in your stomach and are very painful. Alcohol can also increase the risk of stomach cancer.

Liver
One job of the **liver** is to process alcohol. Too much alcohol destroys liver cells causing cancer, **cirrhosis** and other diseases that can kill.

Groin
Too much alcohol can make it difficult for a man to get an **erection**.

Too bad
Kelli and Deb were going to see their favourite band. Kelli was ready to go when she got a text message.

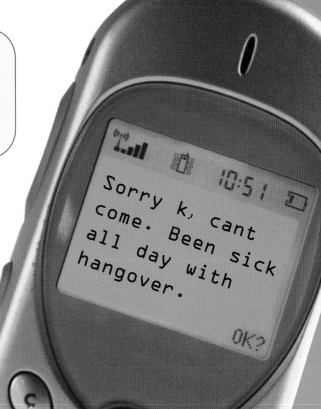

Sorry k. cant come. Been sick all day with hangover.

OK?

---

heart disease damage to the heart which stops it working properly

Alcohol and your brain

Can alcohol affect your school work? Yes, because alcohol affects your memory. Scientific research suggests alcohol can make it difficult for you to learn new information. This is bad news if you are studying. In fact, it is a double problem, because when the brain is affected by alcohol it makes more mistakes *and* it becomes less likely to notice them.

Sounds awful

Ever wondered why people sing so badly when they are drunk? It is partly because alcohol's impact on the brain makes it more difficult for people to sing or play in tune, even if they are usually good musicians.

We sound great!

alcoholic   someone who is addicted to (cannot manage without) alcohol

Alcohol slows the brain down sooner and for longer than most people think. People can make mistakes they do not even notice after just a small amount of alcohol. This small amount can be a lot less than the **legal** limit for driving.

Life and death

Alcohol may help people go to sleep, but it disrupts the brain's natural sleep patterns. This means they will not have a very good night's sleep. Even if they do not wake up in the night, they will not feel rested in the morning. The brain does not work as well if it is tired.

Regular drinking can damage your brain. So can drinking a lot in one go. This is sometimes called **binge-drinking** and it is very dangerous. It is especially dangerous for young people, because their brains are more sensitive. People can die from binge-drinking and then **choking** on their own vomit.

I can't remember getting home last night. In fact, I can't remember where I went after the bar.

binge-drinking   drinking a lot of alcohol in a short space of time
choke   when you cannot breathe because something is blocking your throat

Alcohol and your liver

The **liver** sits inside the bottom of your rib cage on the right-hand side. It weighs about 1.5 kilograms, so it is quite big. Its job is to make sure the body has all the chemicals it needs in the right amounts.

Even after just a few alcoholic drinks, your liver can feel sore and painful the next day. Imagine how it must feel if you regularly binge on alcohol.

▼ The holes in this section of liver were caused by cirrhosis.

Q&A

Q Why do I feel so hungover?

A Alcohol reduces the amount of water in your brain and body, and this causes headaches. If you are sick you will get even more **dehydrated**. Alcohol also disrupts your sleep and, of course, your stomach and liver. Add these up and you have a nasty hangover.

dehydrated not enough water (fluids) in your body
inflamed bigger and quite sore

Facts

▶ 80 per cent of liver disease is caused by alcohol.

▶ Liver disease is getting more common. In the UK, the number of people with liver disease is dramatically rising.

▶ Liver disease does some strange things. It can disrupt the body's hormones so men may grow breasts and lose hair.

What can happen

Alcohol kills liver cells making the liver fatty and **inflamed**. If someone with a fatty, inflamed liver carries on drinking, their liver can become permanently scarred. This is called **cirrhosis** (sear-osis). Cirrhosis kills.

People with liver disease should stop drinking alcohol and start to eat healthy foods that help the liver work. If this does not help, a liver **transplant** may be needed. But this is not always possible because it is very hard to find a donated liver. Also, the transplant operation itself can be dangerous and does not always work.

Think about this…

Binge-drinking causes alcohol poisoning and can make you pass out. In the UK around 1000 people under fifteen are taken to hospital with alcohol poisoning each year. Many need intensive care. Some even die.

transplant   replacing an organ like a liver or heart with one donated (given) from someone else's body

Alcohol and your looks

It is not just the insides of your body that can be damaged if you keep drinking too much alcohol. Cindy found that it affected her appearance, too.

Weighty problem

Alcohol is fattening. It is made from sugar, remember! A pint of beer contains about 185 **calories** – 30 calories more than a 28 gram packet of crisps. A glass of sweet wine contains 120 calories – nearly as many as half a bar of chocolate.

> Drinking alcohol made me feel more grown-up. My boyfriend was older than me and he used to encourage it. It made me feel more confident and even more attractive. But to be honest that doesn't last long. Soon I was only thinking about drinking – not going-out, not friends, not school, not even my boyfriend, nothing. He dumped me and that made me drink even more.

banned   stopped from doing something

My hangovers in the morning got worse. Sometimes I didn't make it in until lunchtime. I got fat and lazy and I was losing contact with people. Friends stopped asking me to their parties. I told myself I wasn't bothered. But I was lying. Really I didn't want to go because I'd lost my confidence and felt fat and ugly. I'd become an embarrassment to myself.

Think about this...

DRINKING TOO MUCH ALCOHOL CAN SERIOUSLY DAMAGE YOUR HEALTH

5% Alcohol

Some countries, like France, have health warnings on posters and magazine adverts about the dangers of alcohol. The warnings are like those on cigarette packets. Many doctors would like alcohol advertising to be **banned** completely.

Alcohol and risks

Alcohol can make you do things you would not normally do. Falling over or being sick is embarrassing. It is even more serious when you start to take risks. This is what happened to Collette.

I met this bloke at a party. I didn't even fancy him. I would never have let him walk me home if I had been sober. I thought I was being so smart. I knew I was drunk and might need help, but all the girls reckoned he was safe. He put his arm around me after about 30 seconds. I should have got the message then, but I thought I could handle it...

virginity   a virgin has never had sex; you lose your virginity the first time you have sex

> The trouble is I can't remember what happened after that. I think we were in the park and I think I did say 'Yes'. My head was spinning and I just wanted to shut him up. I'm sure he said he was using a **condom**, but I can't really remember. I can't even remember getting home. It was only when I saw the grass all over my jacket the next morning that it started coming back to me. God, I was so stupid. Now I'm having a baby and I will never be able to forget it.

One in four boys and one in five girls lose their **virginity** or have a one-night-stand they regret when they are drunk.

Q&A

Q What are 'date rape' drugs?

A These are drugs that can be put in someone's drink to make them tired, unable to think and forgetful. Most of the drugs are **illegal**. People can go to prison for putting them in drinks.

condom   thin rubber protection worn on the penis during sex
sober   not drunk

'A small amount of alcohol is good for some people.'

TRUE

For older people, drinking a small amount of alcohol can protect them against **heart disease**, a **stroke** and stress. But in people under 45 years old, there is no benefit.

Safe amounts to drink

Most **governments** give advice on safe drinking. This is advice for adults. Do not forget that younger people can be damaged much more by alcohol than adults because their bodies are still growing and developing. The advice below is based on safe-drinking guidelines for adults. Remember, a unit of alcohol is about half a pint of beer (see page 16).

- Women (over eighteen) should drink no more than two to three units a day.
- Men (over eighteen) should drink no more than three to four units a day.
- It is not a good idea to drink every day. Adults are advised not to drink on at least two days out of every week.
- Avoid **binge-drinking**.

The guidelines

When it comes to alcohol, it is hard to say exactly how much is too much. Some people are less affected by alcohol than others. But some people may even have problems when they stick to the safe-drinking guidelines. It also depends on age and size. A small amount for an adult is a large amount for a child.

There is a high risk of danger to young people who have unsafe drinking habits. For example, it is a bad idea to drink on an empty stomach or to mix alcohol with other drugs. Drinking a lot of units in a short period of time also increases the danger.

Q Who might have a drink problem?

A All kinds of people can have a drink problem. Alcohol is not just a problem for people you see sleeping rough. It can affect anyone, of any age, sex or class.

◀ It is a good idea to alternate **soft drinks** and alcoholic drinks.

Alcohol does not just affect the people who drink it. It can also have effects on their family, friends and other people around them.

Drunk teacher sacked

A school teacher was fired yesterday after making mistakes that led to thousands of students being given the wrong examination results. The teacher admitted to being drunk while marking examination papers. He said, 'I was under a lot of pressure and working extra hours because of the new marking schemes. The only way I could keep going was with a drink.'

The teacher did not notice that he was marking out of 50 instead of 100, so students were being awarded half the marks they should have been.

fatal accident   accident in which someone has been killed

How would you feel?

How would you feel if the teacher in the news story had marked your exam paper? His drunken mistake would have affected many young people. But at least nobody died, which is what can happen in some workplaces if people are drunk.

Think about what could happen on a building site or in a hospital or factory, for example. One in four accidents at work are caused by alcohol. One in five **fatal accidents** at work are caused by alcohol.

▼ How much you drink is not the only issue. Think about where you are drinking and who else you could be affecting.

TRUE OR FALSE?

'Alcohol affects everyone in a different way.'

TRUE

Your age, size and the way your body works all make a difference. So does the time of day, whether you are feeling happy or sad and why you are choosing to have a drink in the first place.

The cost of alcohol

Too much alcohol can lead to much more than a few nasty hangovers.

▲ What else could you be spending that money on?

> Alcohol can lead to accidents including; drownings, fires, car accidents, **assaults** and accidents in the home.

> Alcohol can lead to crime. It is estimated that about 30 per cent of sexual **offenders** are 'under the influence of alcohol'. So are 33 per cent of people who break into houses and 50 per cent of muggers and other street offenders.

> Alcohol can lead to violence. The British Crime **Survey** reports that 40 per cent of violent crimes in the UK involve alcohol.

> Alcohol can lead to **poverty**. To pay for alcohol, people sometimes have to stop paying for food, electricity and housing.

Think about this...

Do you know how much a beer in a bar costs? Work out how expensive it could get if you were buying several beers a day. Spirits are even more expensive.

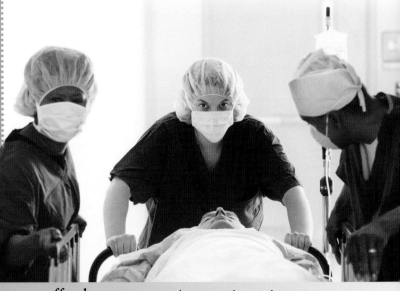

offender   someone who commits a crime
poverty   being poor

Online answers

Harry was getting worried about his father's drinking and emailed a men's health website for help.

▶▶▶▶▶▶▶▶▶

Go to pages 52 to 53 to find out about organizations that can help with drinking problems.

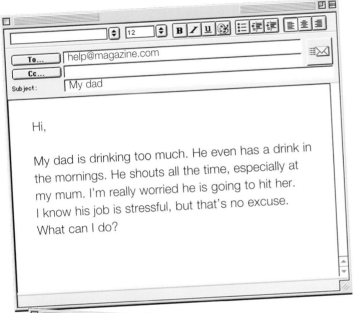

To... help@magazine.com
Cc...
Subject: My dad

Hi,

My dad is drinking too much. He even has a drink in the mornings. He shouts all the time, especially at my mum. I'm really worried he is going to hit her. I know his job is stressful, but that's no excuse. What can I do?

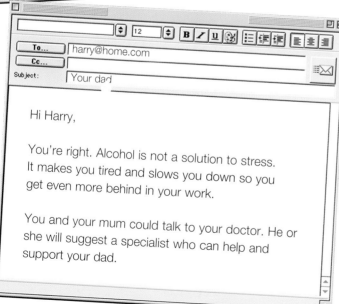

To... harry@home.com
Cc...
Subject: Your dad

Hi Harry,

You're right. Alcohol is not a solution to stress. It makes you tired and slows you down so you get even more behind in your work.

You and your mum could talk to your doctor. He or she will suggest a specialist who can help and support your dad.

Violent drinkers

Even gentle people can become violent if they drink too much for too long. They often feel guilty when they are **sober** and promise not to be violent again. But alcohol changes them and next time they are drunk they will probably be violent again.

▼ If you live with a violent drinker, tell someone. Get help.

Alcohol and relationships

Drunk people are sometimes funny, but not for long. Most of us get fed up with people who are always drunk. Heavy drinkers have problems keeping family, friends, boyfriends and girlfriends.

Ed was tired of his girlfriend's drinking. He emailed his friend Sara about it.

TRUE OR FALSE?

'Clear drinks are better than dark-coloured drinks.'

FALSE

In general what counts is how much alcohol you drink, not what colour the drink is. But darker-coloured liquids can sometimes make you feel worse the next morning.

culture   customs, practices and beliefs of a group of people

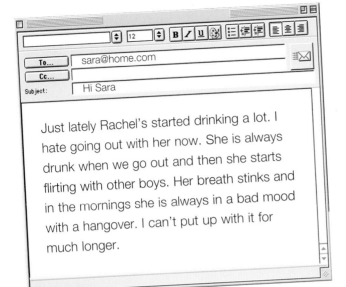

To... sara@home.com

Cc...

Subject: Hi Sara

Just lately Rachel's started drinking a lot. I hate going out with her now. She is always drunk when we go out and then she starts flirting with other boys. Her breath stinks and in the mornings she is always in a bad mood with a hangover. I can't put up with it for much longer.

To... ed@home.com

Cc...

Subject: Hi Ed

Tell me about it! My boyfriend gets drunk and then he will not stop talking. It's so boring and he doesn't listen to what I'm saying. Then he plays these stupid drinking games with his mates. He never wants to go out anywhere but the bar. He used to look so cool but his skin is awful now and he is fat. What's worse, he has nothing interesting to say to me anymore. Fancy going to see a film with me tonight?

Culture shock

Different countries have different attitudes to drunkenness. In summer 2003, a British girl got drunk and took off her bra in a bar in Greece. She was arrested and could have spent eight months in prison.

▶ It is important to respect other people's **cultures** and drink carefully when you are on holiday abroad.

Drinking and driving

In Europe, men and women who drive when drunk kill over 10,000 people every year. That is more than one death an hour.

It is **illegal** to drive with too much alcohol in your body. But what is too much? In the UK and Ireland, the limit is 0.8 milligrams of alcohol per millilitre of blood. In Australia, the **legal** limit is 0.5 milligrams of alcohol per millilitre of blood. Many people think there would be fewer deaths from drink-driving in the UK if the limit was lowered to 0.5.

Drink-driving is a very serious **offence**. People can be fined, **banned** from driving and put in prison for many years.

▼ There is still a long way to go before drink driving is stamped out altogether.

offence   a crime

A very real tragedy

Four people waiting at a bus stop were killed last Thursday when a car flew off the road and crashed into them. A passenger in the car was also killed. Only the driver survived. He is being treated in hospital for his injuries.

Police have confirmed that the driver was over the legal limit for alcohol when he crashed the car. He is due to appear in court next week charged with causing death by dangerous driving. If found guilty he could face a long prison sentence.

Q&A

Q What is a breathalyser?

A A breathalyser measures the alcohol level in your breath. The police use it to find out if you are drunk while driving. The driver has to blow into a machine, which tells the police whether he or she has drunk more than the legal limit.

Warning signs

It can be difficult to tell if someone is drinking too much. But there are a few signs you can look for if you are worried that a friend or family member has an alcohol problem.

Are they drinking every day?

Do they drink in the morning?

Are they drinking alone or secretly?

Are they drinking regularly at certain times (for example, after coming back from school or work)?

Do they get angry when their drinking is mentioned, try to deny it or laugh it off?

Is drinking spoiling their work?

Is drinking making them aggressive or grumpy?

Alcoholics Anonymous (AA) group that helps people with alcohol problems

Who can help?

When Robert was worried about his mother's drinking, he decided it was important to talk to someone.

> My mum always had an excuse for drinking. She drank because it was Christmas or her birthday – or for any reason she could think of. Then she lost her job and she said she had to drink to cheer herself up.

> I'd heard about **Alcoholics Anonymous**, so I looked them up on the Internet. They put me in touch with a local group that works with families. It really helps to know we're not alone. I've always got people who will help me talk to mum in the best way.

Think about this...

In Victoria, Australia, new drivers are not allowed to drive with any alcohol in their blood at all. This law mainly affects young drivers. Some people would like to see laws like this in the UK and other European countries.

Reasons for not drinking

Some people do not drink for religious reasons. Different religions have different views on alcohol. Most religions are against people drinking too much and some are against any use of alcohol at all. But it is always a personal choice. It is not unusual for people who share the same religion to have different views on drinking alcohol. For example, Methodists and Catholics are all Christians. But while most Methodists do not drink, many Catholics do.

A matter of taste

It is interesting to hear different people's opinions about alcohol. What do you and your friends think?

It's simple. I don't drink because I don't like it. It tastes horrible. Some people might want to blur reality, but I don't. I want to stay sharp. It's a beautiful world. Who wants to look at it through a fog?

Koran   holy book of the Islam religion
scripture   the sacred (holy) writings of a religion

Different viewpoints

I'm a Hindu. Hindu **scripture** is against drinking.

I'm Jewish. I have a glass of wine sometimes because wine is a symbol of joy to Jews. Our holy book The **Talmud** teaches sensible moderation. We believe both extremes – not drinking at all or drinking too much – are harmful.

You decide

It is your choice. If you do not want to drink alcohol nobody has the right to make you!

I'm a Christian, so I have wine every Sunday in church. Jesus also turned water into wine, so obviously I can't see any problem with alcohol. Drunkenness is the problem, not drinking.

I'm a Muslim and our holy book The **Koran** says that when it comes to alcohol the sin outweighs the benefit. From what I've seen in our local bar, that's spot on. I stick to juice.

Talmud   holy book of the Jewish religion

Just one alcoholic drink makes it harder for the heart to get blood and oxygen to the rest of the body.

▶ You need to work hard and stay focused if you want to compete to the best of your ability.

Alcohol and sport

Some people do not drink because of their health or for other reasons. Serena and Venus Williams are two of the greatest female tennis players ever. They do not drink and have made films encouraging young people not to take drugs like alcohol. The sisters put it simply: 'Drugs kill dreams'.

Sports players often do not drink because alcohol ruins their performance. In the past, some footballers used to drink a lot, but not now. Modern football is so competitive that you can only play it if you are at your very best. David Beckham is happy to tell anyone that he does not drink very much alcohol.

professional   someone who does something as a job, not just as a hobby

Drunk men can't jump

It is not just **professional** sports players who do not drink. You may not be able to play like Beckham, but you can copy his attitude to alcohol. Tommy plays basketball for his local team.

❛ Why don't I drink? Because drunk men can't jump. Alcohol just makes you feel slow and sluggish. Basketball's a fast game. I need my legs and brain to work fast. You can see when players have had too much to drink the night before. My coach says alcohol reduces the efficiency of your heart, your lungs and your muscles. When you know that, the choice is obvious. ❜

45

Beer is definitely not good for babies. In the past, some mums who were breast-feeding their babies used to drink stout because stout beers are high in **iron**.

Alcohol and pregnancy

Most pregnant women do not drink because alcohol can affect the unborn baby.
A pregnant mother and her baby share the same blood supply. So, if the mother drinks a lot of alcohol so does her baby. But because the baby is a lot smaller, the impact is a lot bigger.

Babies whose mums drink a lot may be born small. Alcohol can affect the development of the **foetus**, especially during the early stages of pregnancy.

▼ Eating a healthy, **balanced diet** will help a woman give her unborn baby the best start in life.

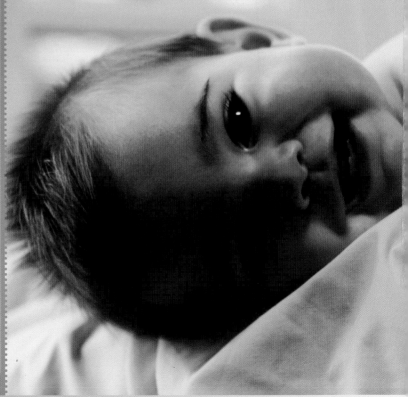

balanced diet   eating a good mixture of foods from all the different food groups

Tori's diary

Tori kept a diary of her pregnancy.

Monday 4th

Decided not to drink alcohol. If more than three units of alcohol is dangerous for a woman of my height and weight, what's safe for a foetus that's a few centimetres long?

Thursday 7th

Spent all day telling myself I can last through my pregnancy without a drink. But it was a hard day to stick to it because of Kirsty and Bill's party. I wasn't looking forward to it because I couldn't drink. But I really enjoyed it. I just danced and danced. Will not be able to do that when I'm bigger. Never noticed before how stupid Kirsty is when she's drunk. Bill looked really embarrassed. Poor bloke.

Q What is foetal alcohol syndrome?

A Women who drink more than six units of alcohol every day risk having babies with foetal alcohol syndrome, or FAS. The brains and bodies of children born with FAS grow more slowly and they have weak hearts.

foetus (or fetus) unborn baby

Alcohol and the law

'In England, you can buy orange juice in a pub when you are fourteen.'

FALSE

You can only go into the pub. You cannot buy any drinks until you are sixteen.

There is no right age to drink alcohol. Different countries have different **age limits**. However, all the laws agree that adults should be able to choose whether or not to drink.

If you choose to drink when you are old enough that is fine. But you must be aware of the effects alcohol can have and be honest with yourself about the effects it is having on you. However sensible you try to be, some people's bodies and brains just cannot handle alcohol. Some may come to depend on it.

In 2002, in the UK, roughly 24 per cent of eleven to fifteen year olds drank at least once a week, even though they were under the legal age limit.

controlled environment   where something is carefully watched and is safe

Legal drinking ages

(5) The age at which parents can let a child drink alcohol in private in the UK. In other parts of Europe many children drink small amounts of alcohol at home.

(14) The age you can enter a bar or licensed premises in the UK. Licensed premises are places where the owner has a licence to sell alcohol. Anybody who sells alcohol must have a licence.

(18) The age you can **legally** buy alcohol in the UK, Australia and many other countries.

(21) The age you can buy alcohol in the USA.

TRUE OR FALSE?

'In the USA, you cannot take Communion in church until you are 21.'

FALSE

Most states make exceptions for religious ceremonies and other **controlled environments**.

Avoiding dangerous drinking

Some things about alcohol are matters of opinion. You need to make up your own mind. But some things are matters of fact. One of the most important facts is that **binge-drinking** is dangerous, especially for young people. When people start to drink, it is a good idea for them to think of ways to avoid drinking too much in one go.

✓ Do not get into big 'rounds' of drinks.

✓ Have a soft drink every so often.

✓ Say 'No' from time to time.

✓ Do not mix different types of drinks. As a rule, the less alcoholic the drink, the better.

✓ Always know how much you have drunk.

✓ Limit yourself to spending a certain amount of money.

Hangover cure

Raw eggs are just one of the cures people try for hangovers. None of them really work. The only way to beat a hangover is not to drink too much alcohol in the first place. Drinking water before going to bed may help make the hangover less unpleasant.

rounds   when everyone buys everyone else a drink in turn

The price of a binge

A night of bingeing can cost a lot of money. This is what it adds up to in **calories**.

6 pints of beer	1092	calories
2 large burgers	1040	calories
fries	360	calories
3 packs of crisps	459	calories
TOTAL	**2951**	**calories**

That number of calories is enough to keep a grown man going for a whole day or more. Let's face it, you are going to feel terrible in the morning after that lot. It is not just your brain that gets damaged, it is your stomach too.

Many people enjoy drinking alcohol. You can too if you want to. But alcohol is a drug and it can be a very dangerous one. It can kill. Now that you know the facts about alcohol you can make your own choice.

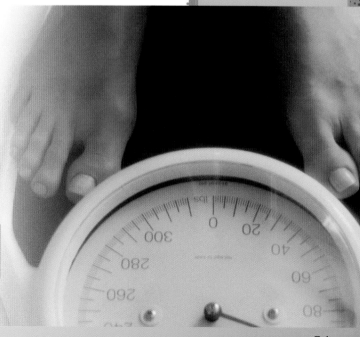

▶ You may notice you put on weight if you drink regularly.

Think about this...

Here are two facts about alcohol:

- It makes you feel hungry.

- It makes you fat.

Put the two together and what have you got? Everybody has seen drinkers with big stomachs, or 'beer bellies'. They are taking a big risk. The fatter you get, the bigger your risk of **heart disease** and other illnesses.

51

Find out more

Organizations

The Australian Drug Foundation

The Australian Drug Foundation has a wide range of information on all aspects of drugs, their effects and their legal position in Australia.
www.adf.org.au

Hope UK

Hope UK educates young people on the problem that alcohol and other drugs cause.
www.hopeuk.org

Lifebytes

A fun and informative website that gives young people information to help them make their own choices about their life.
www.lifebytes.gov.uk

Male Health

A good source of essential information about key health issues that affect men.
www.malehealth.co.uk

Books

Learn to say no: Alcohol, Angela Royston (Heinemann Library, 2000)

Need to know: Alcohol, Sean Connolly (Heinemann Library, 2001)

What's at issue: Drugs and you, Bridget Lawless (Heinemann Library, 1999)

World Wide Web

If you want to find out more about **alcohol**, you can search the Internet using keywords like these:
- alcohol + abuse
- 'liver damage'
- drugs
- binge + drinking

You can also find your own keywords by using headings or words from this book. Use the search tips opposite to help you find the most useful websites.

Search tips

There are billions of pages on the Internet so it can be difficult to find exactly what you are looking for. For example, if you just type in 'alcohol' on a search engine like Google, you'll get a list of over 10 million web pages. These search skills will help you find useful websites more quickly:

- Know exactly what you want to find out about first
- Use simple keywords instead of whole sentences
- Use two to six keywords in a search, putting the most important words first
- Be precise – only use names of people, places or things
- If you want to find words that go together, put quote marks around them, for example 'binge drinking' or 'alcohol addiction'
- Use the advanced section of your search engine.

Where to search

Search engine
A search engine looks through the web and lists the sites that match the words in the search box. They can give thousands of links, but the best matches are at the top of the list, on the first page. Try searching with www.bbc.co.uk/search

Search directory
A search directory is like a library of websites. You can search by keyword or subject and browse through the different sites like you would look through books on a library shelf. A good example is www.yahooligans.com

Glossary

absorb soak up

age limit legal age when you can start drinking alcohol

alcoholic someone who is addicted to (cannot manage without) alcohol

Alcoholics Anonymous (AA) group that helps people with alcohol problems

assault attack

balanced diet eating a good mixture of food from all the different food groups

banned stopped from doing something

binge-drinking drinking a lot of alcohol in a short space of time

blackout sudden loss of memory

brewery factory where beer is made

calorie measures the energy value of food

champagne fizzy alcoholic drink made from grapes

choke when you cannot breathe because something is blocking your throat

cirrhosis when the liver becomes scarred

condom thin rubber protection worn on the penis during sex

controlled environment where something is carefully watched and is safe

culture customs, practices and beliefs of a group of people

dehydrated not enough water (fluids) in your body

depressant something that slows you down

distillery place where spirits are made

erection stiffening and enlarging of the penis when sexually excited

fatal accident accident in which someone has been killed

fermentation changing sugar to alcohol by adding yeast

foetus (or fetus) unborn baby

government group of people in charge of the country

heart disease damage to the heart which stops it working properly

heroin powerful and addictive drug

Holy Communion ceremony in which bread and wine are blessed and shared

illegal against the law

inflamed bigger and quite sore

iron your blood needs this to be healthy

Islam the religion of Muslims

Koran holy book of the Islam religion

lager type of beer

legal within the law

liver part of the body turning the nutrients from food and drink into the proteins and sugars the body needs

offence a crime

offender someone who commits a crime

optic something fixed on the top of a bottle so that it pours out the same measure each time; usually made of clear plastic

poverty being poor

professional someone who does something as a job, not just as a hobby

rounds when everyone buys everyone else a drink in turn

scripture sacred (holy) writings of a religion

sober not drunk

soft drinks drinks that do not contain alcohol, like orange juice and cola

stroke when the blood flow to part of the brain is blocked

survey research that gives you information

Talmud holy book of the Jewish religion

transplant replacing an organ like a liver or heart with one donated (given) from someone else's body

virginity a virgin has never had sex; you lose your virginity the first time you have sex

Index